CAROLYN ROSSI COPELAND   ALEXANDER RANKIN
AG FUNDING LLC
present

JOSH YOUNG   ERIN MACKEY
in

AMAZING GRACE

T0070688

Music & Lyrics by
CHRISTOPHER SMITH

Book by
CHRISTOPHER SMITH
and ARTHUR GIRON

With

TOM HEWITT   CHUCK COOPER   CHRIS HOCH
STANLEY BAHOREK   HARRIETT D. FOY   LAIONA MICHELLE
RACHAEL FERRERA   ELIZABETH WARD LAND

LESLIE BECKER   SARA BROPHY   RHEAUME CRENSHAW   MIQUEL EDSON
MIKE EVARISTE   SEAN EWING   SAVANNAH FRAZIER   CHRISTOPHER GURR
ALLEN KENDALL   MICHAEL DEAN MORGAN   VINCE ODDO   ONEIKA PHILLIPS
CLIFTON SAMUELS   GAVRIEL SAVIT   DAN SHARKEY   BRET SHUFORD
EVAN ALEXANDER SMITH   UYOATA UDI   CHARLES E. WALLACE
TONI ELIZABETH WHITE   HOLLIE E. WRIGHT

Scenic Design	*Costume Design*	*Lighting Design*	*Sound Design*
EUGENE LEE	TONI-LESLIE JAMES	KEN BILLINGTON	JON WESTON
EDWARD PIERCE		& PAUL MILLER	

Hair Design
ROBERT-CHARLES VALLANCE

Fight & Military Movement
DAVID LEONG

Casting
McCORKLE CASTING LTD.

Orchestrations
KENNY SEYMOUR

Music Coordinator
MICHAEL KELLER

Dialect Coach
GILLIAN LANE-PLESCIA

Press Representative
BONEAU/
BRYAN-BROWN

Advertising
SPOTCO

Marketing & Social Media
THE PEKOE GROUP

Community Engagement
MARCIA PENDELTON/
WTG PRODUCTIONS

Associate Director
KIM WEILD

Associate Choreographer
SHANNA VANDERWERKER

Company Manager
CHRIS ANIELLO

Production Management
AURORA PRODUCTIONS

General Management
MARSHALL B. PURDY

Production Stage Manager
PAUL J. SMITH

Music Direction, Arrangements & Incidental Music
JOSEPH CHURCH

Choreography by
CHRISTOPHER GATTELLI

Directed by
GABRIEL BARRE

Originally produced by Goodspeed Musicals
Michael P. Price, Executive Producer

Additional material by: Karen Burgman, Dr. Joseph Ohrt, Alana K. Smith, Dr. Sarah Gulish

ISBN 978-1-4950-5816-5

7777 W. BLUEMOUND RD. P.O. BOX 13819 MILWAUKEE, WI 53213

In Australia Contact:
Hal Leonard Australia Pty. Ltd.
4 Lentara Court
Cheltenham, Victoria, 3192 Australia
Email: ausadmin@halleonard.com.au

Visit Hal Leonard Online at
www.halleonard.com

TRULY ALIVE

Music and Lyrics by CHRISTOPHER SMITH
Arranged by Joseph Church

Allegro molto ($\quad$ = 108)

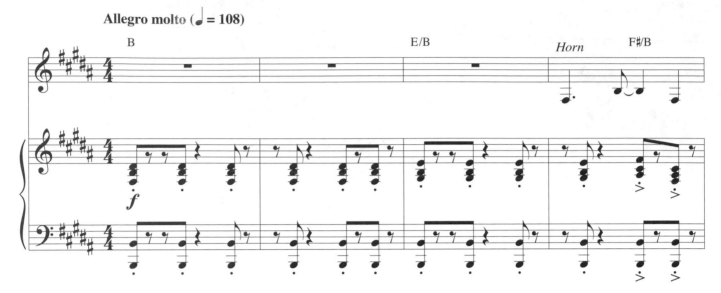

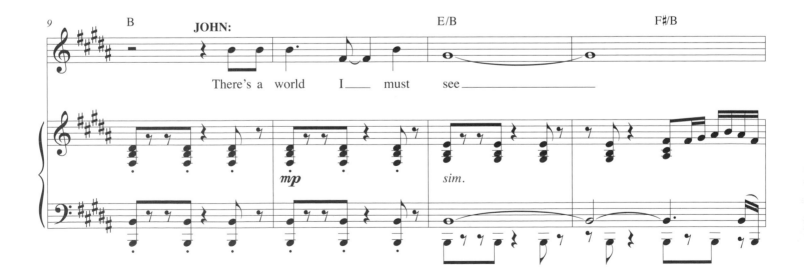

There's a world I___ must see _____

JOHN:

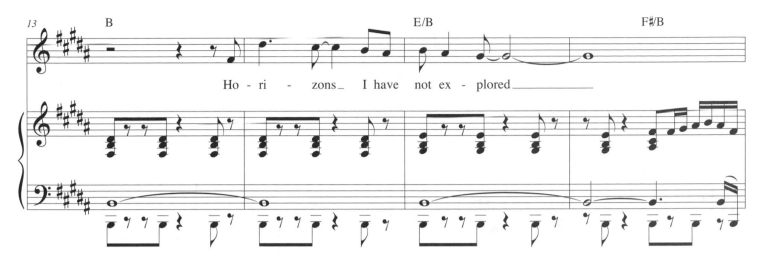

Ho - ri - zons _ I have not ex - plored _____

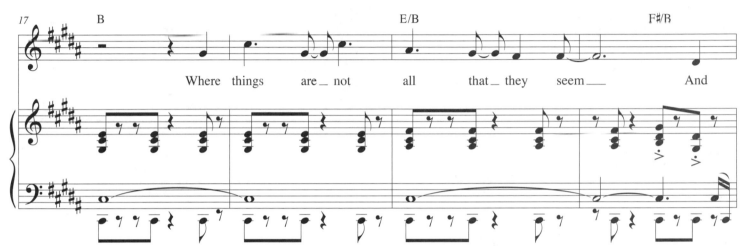

Where things are _ not all that _ they seem _____ And

cour - age _____ is its own _ re - ward _____

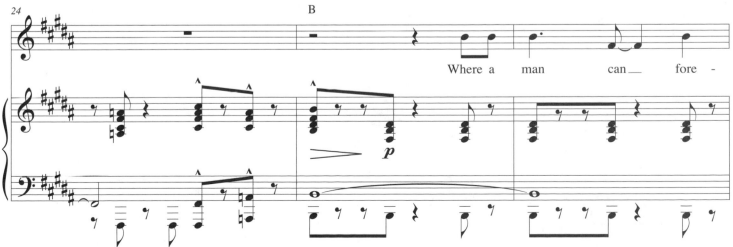

Where a man can _ fore -

life   I   call   my   own _____   It's   up   to

me   to   de - cide   what   I   need _____

to   be   tru - ly ___ a - live. _____

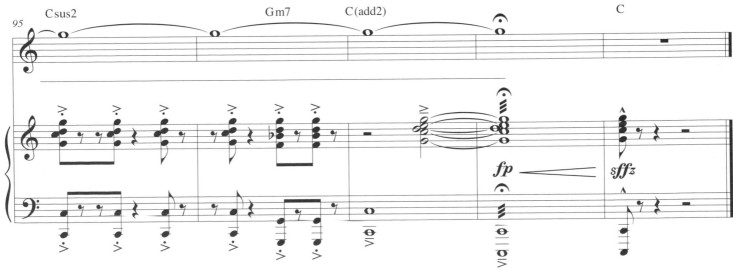

SOMEONE WHO HEARS

Music by CHRISTOPHER SMITH and DR. SARAH GULISH
Lyrics by CHRISTOPHER SMITH
Arranged by Joseph Church
Additional arrangements by Karen Burgman

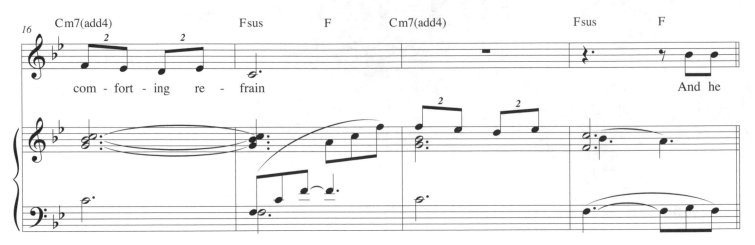

com - fort - ing re - frain And he

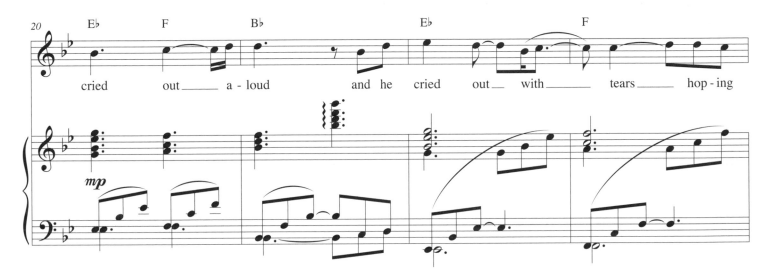

cried out____ a - loud and he cried out__ with____ tears____ hop - ing

some - where____ far be - yond the clouds he'd find some - one who hears Some-

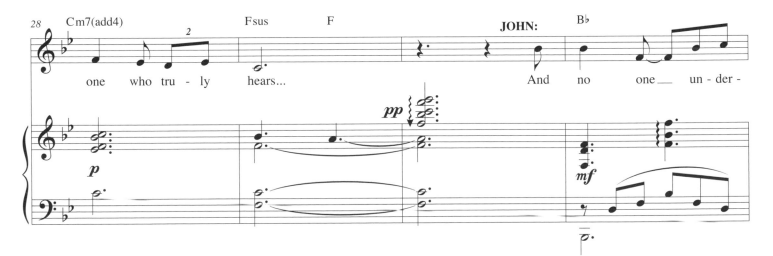

one who tru - ly hears... **JOHN:** And no one____ un - der-

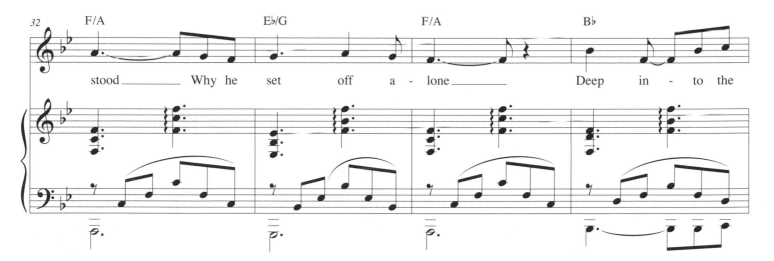

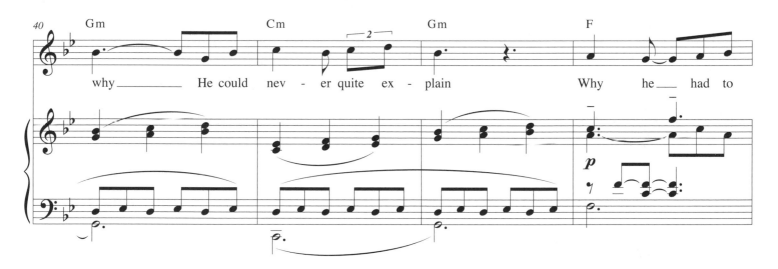

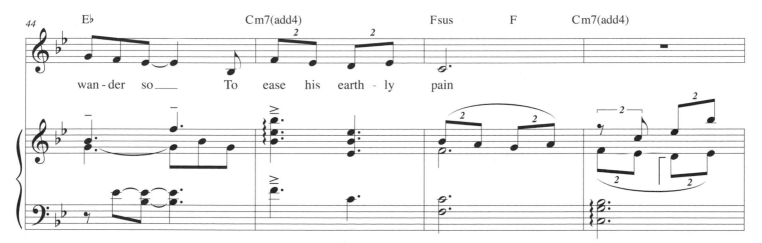

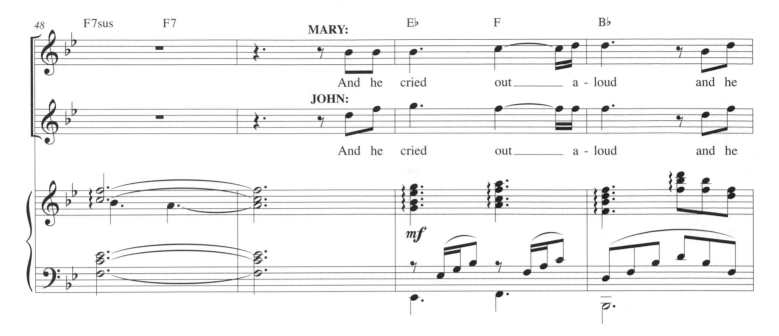

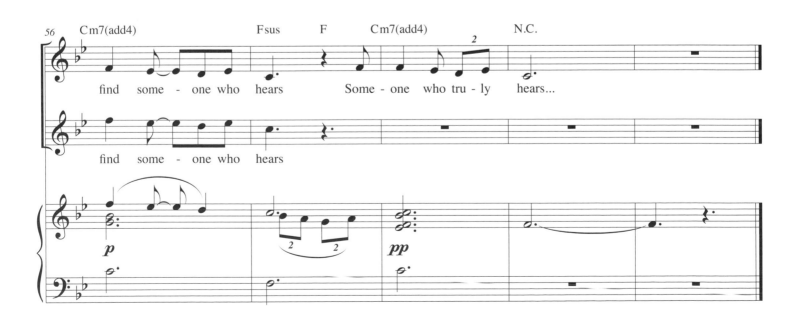

YEMA'S SONG

Music and Lyrics by CHRISTOPHER SMITH
Arranged by Joseph Church

VOICES OF THE ANGELS

Music and Lyrics by CHRISTOPHER SMITH
Arranged by Joseph Church

Molto moderato, Handelian (♩ = 104)

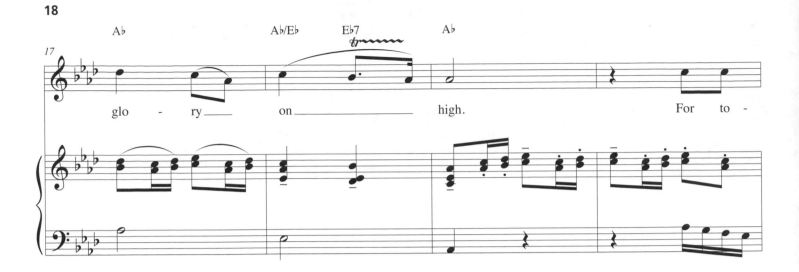

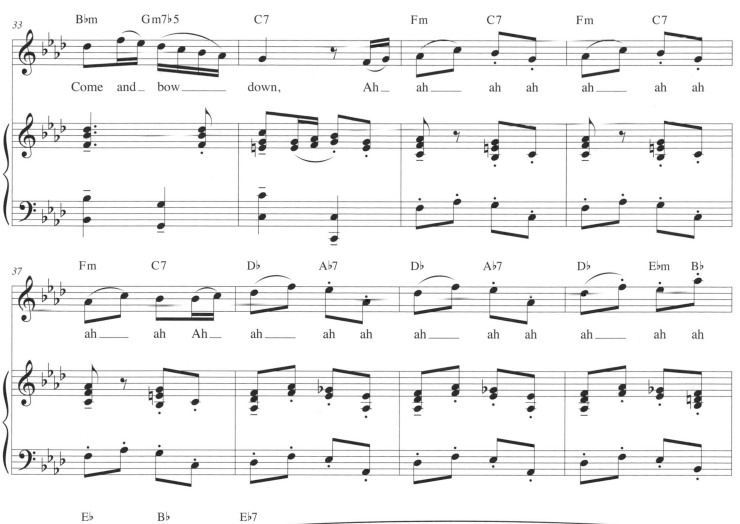

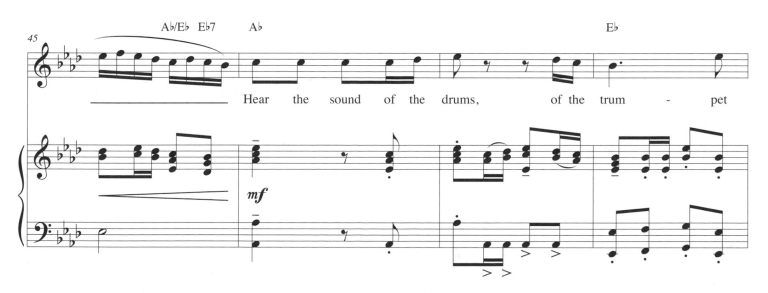

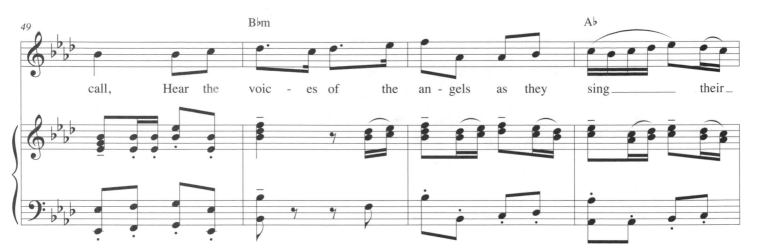

call, Hear the voic - es of the an - gels as they sing_____ their

song, Hal - le - lu - jah,_____ Hal - le - lu - jah,_____

_____ Sing glo - ry,_____ Sing glo - ry_____

on_____ high._____

a tempo   *rit.*

WE ARE DETERMINED

Music and Lyrics by CHRISTOPHER SMITH
Arranged by Joseph Church
Additional arrangements by Dr. Joseph Ohrt

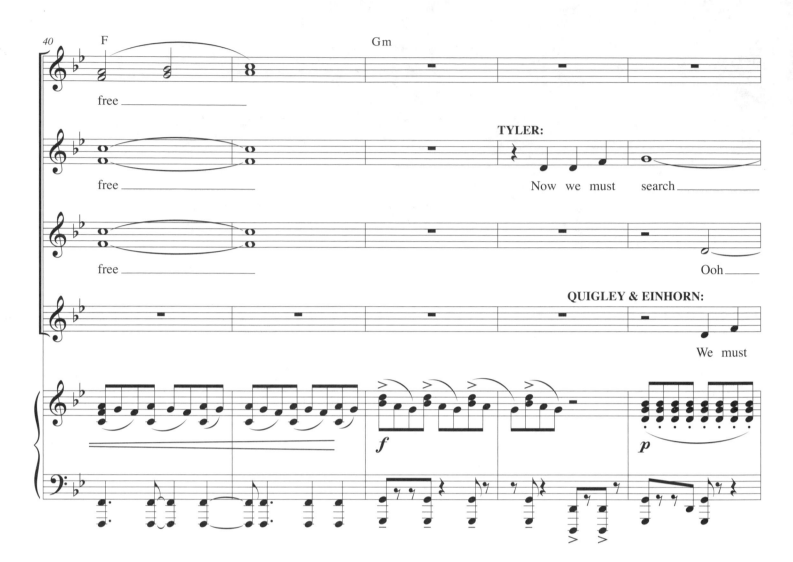

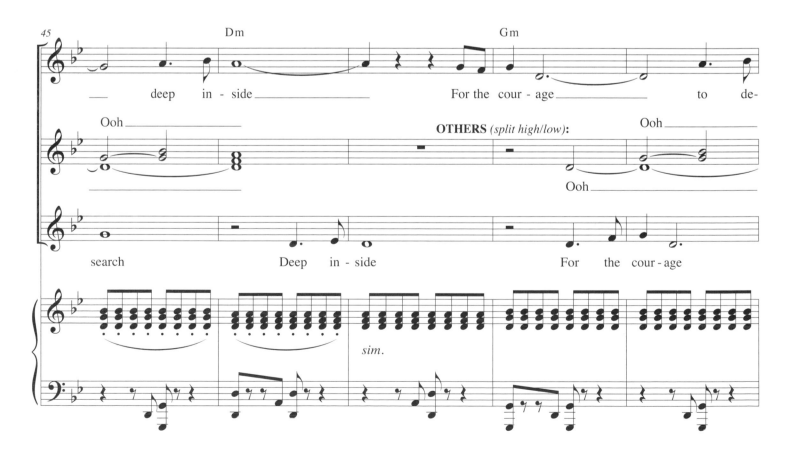

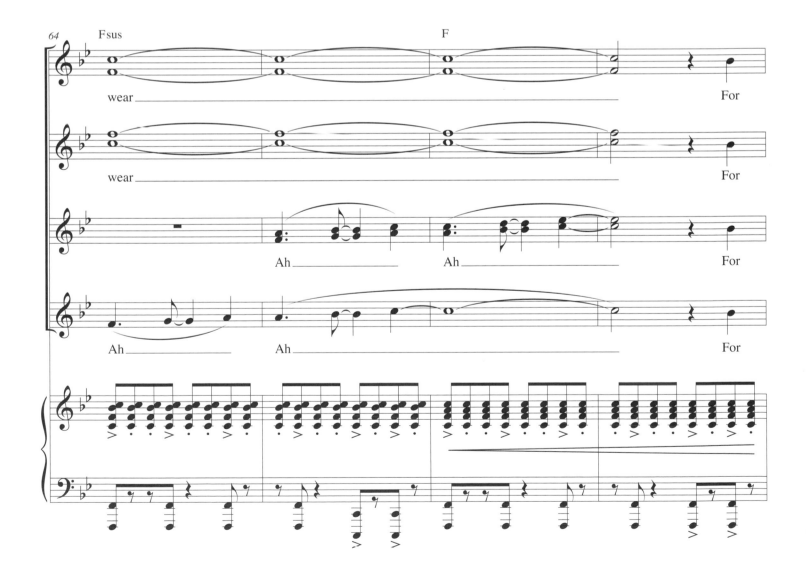

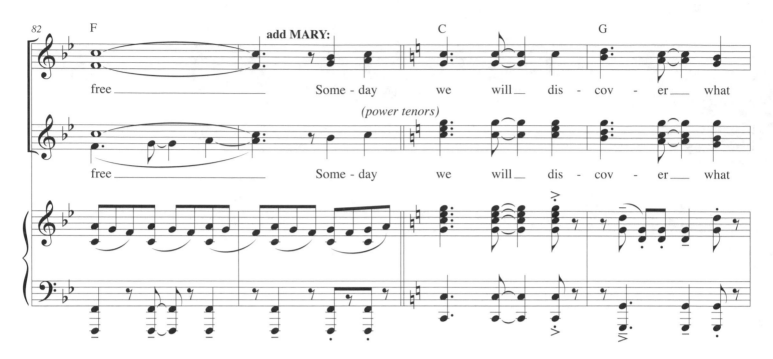

SHADOWS OF INNOCENCE

Music and Lyrics by CHRISTOPHER SMITH
Arranged by Joseph Church
Additional arrangements by Karen Burgman and Alana K. Smith

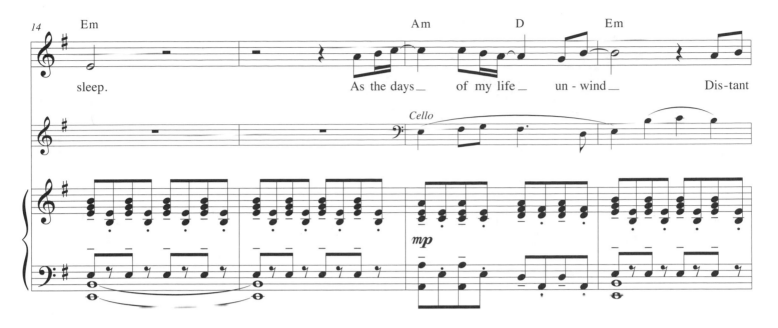

ech - oes of _____ my on-ly chance for love _____ And the peace I long to

MEN: Ooh _____

dolcissimo

find. Can I ev - er ex-plain _____ Long-ing for a man _____

poco legato

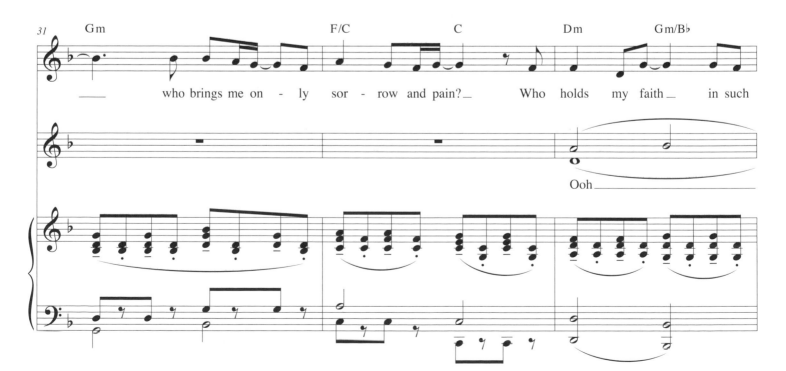

_____ who brings me on - ly sor - row and pain? _____ Who holds my faith _____ in such

Ooh _____

EXPECTATIONS

Music by CHRISTOPHER SMITH
Lyrics by CHRISTOPHER SMITH and ALANA K. SMITH
Arranged by Joseph Church
Additional arrangements by Karen Burgman

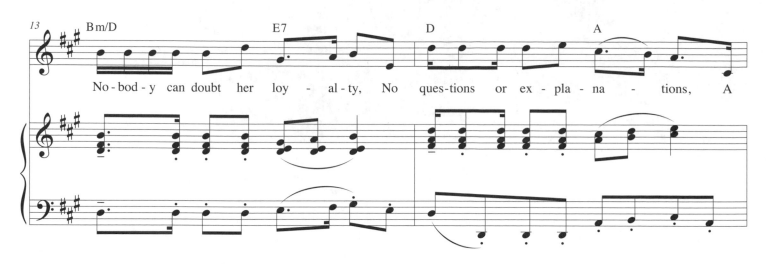

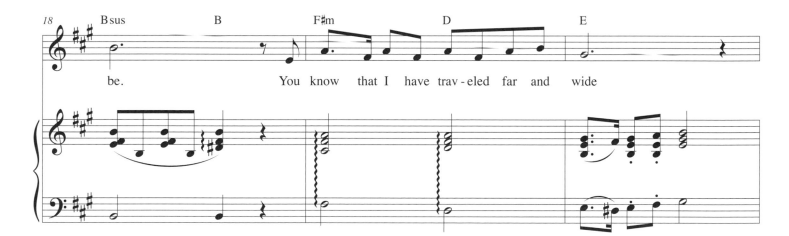

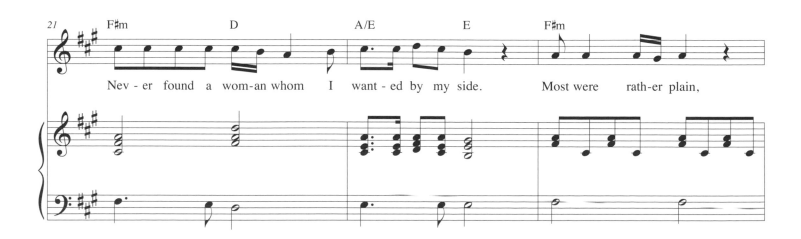

no one else___ ful-fills my stand-ards quite the way___ you do,___ And

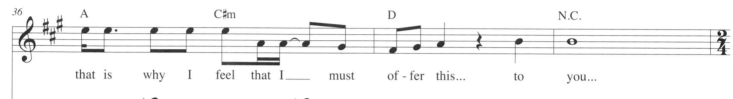

that is why I feel that I___ must of-fer this... to you...

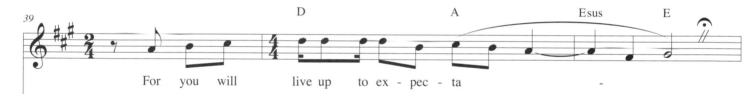

For you will live up to ex-pec-ta -

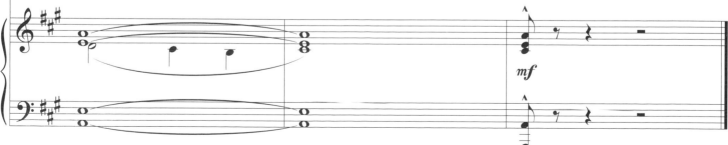

tions!_____

TELL ME WHY

Music and Lyrics by CHRISTOPHER SMITH
Arranged by Joseph Church

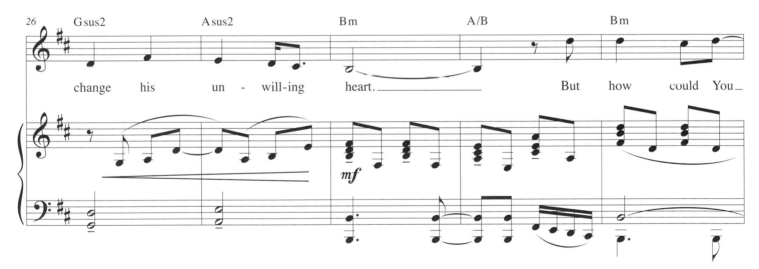

lit this fi - re in_____ my soul_____ for him_____

_____ Why?_____ On - ly to de - ny_____ the

chance_____ to share a life_____ Tell_

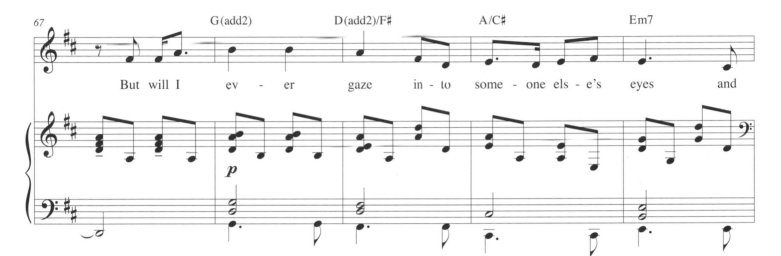

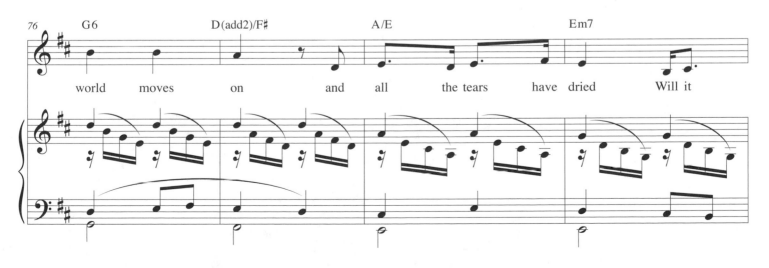

46

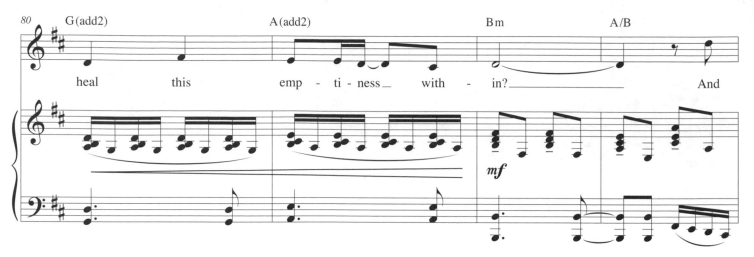

A CHANCE FOR ME

Music by CHRISTOPHER SMITH and KAREN BURGMAN
Lyrics by CHRISTOPHER SMITH
Arranged by Joseph Church

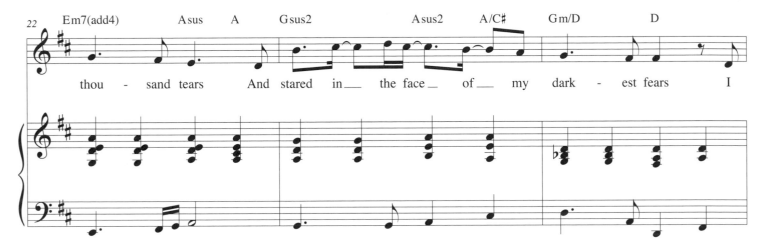

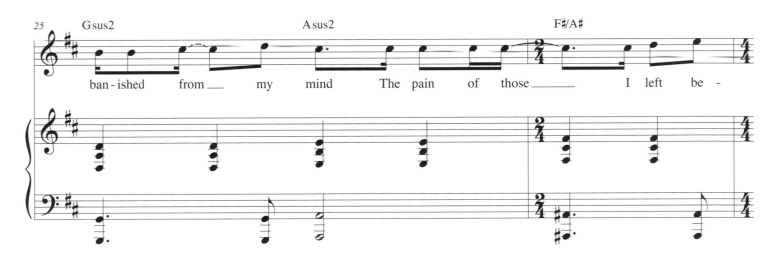

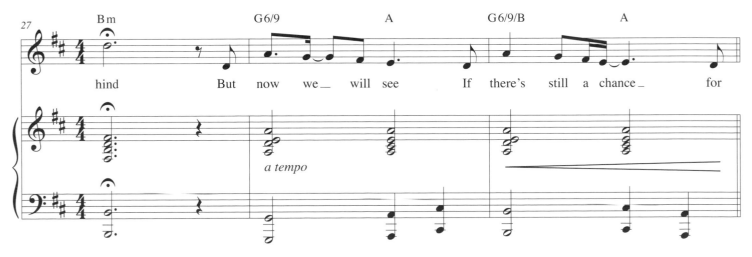

Measured and martial (still ♩ = 80)

NOWHERE LEFT TO RUN

Music and Lyrics by CHRISTOPHER SMITH
Arranged by Joseph Church

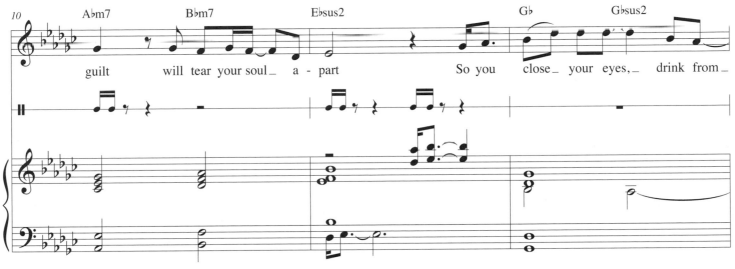

things that just__ won't last____ And none of them__ can ev - er heal your__

__ shame.____

__ Be-cause sin is on - ly good__ for a sea-

DAYBREAK

Music and Lyrics by CHRISTOPHER SMITH
Arranged by Joseph Church
Additional arrangements by Karen Burgman

As the birds start to sing a hymn_____ prais - ing

dark - ness yield - ing to light_____ and a new day

slow - ly be - gins_____ soon the sun_____ is shin - ing

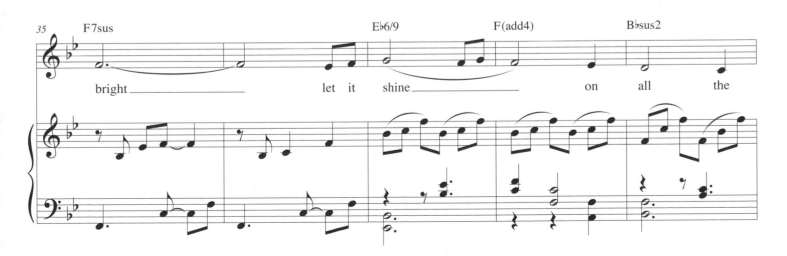

bright_____ let it shine_____ on all the

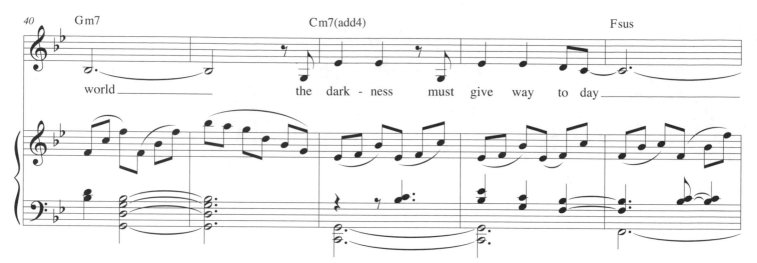

world_____ the dark-ness must give way to day_____

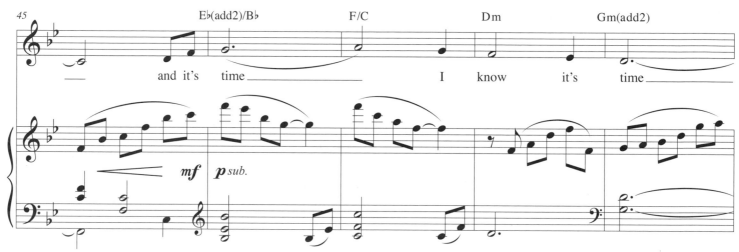

___ and it's time_____ I know it's time_____

_____ these fears that have shak-en our__ faith_____ fade a-

Driving, a bit faster

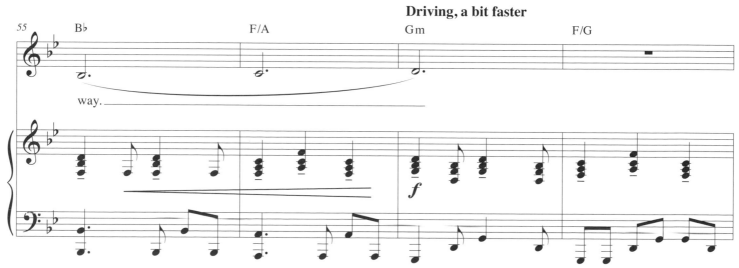

way._____

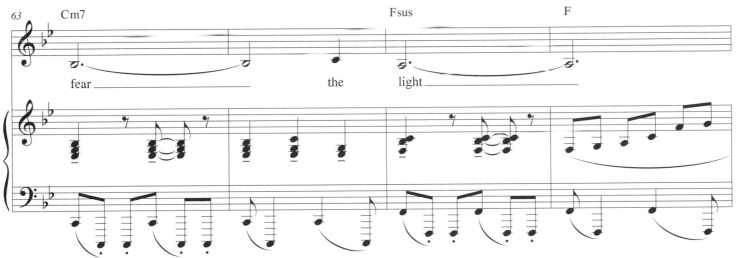

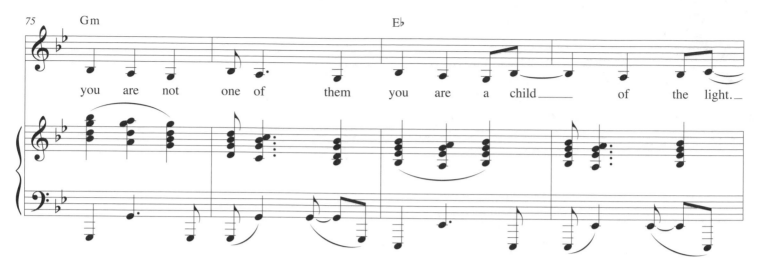

you are not one of them you are a child_____ of the light.___

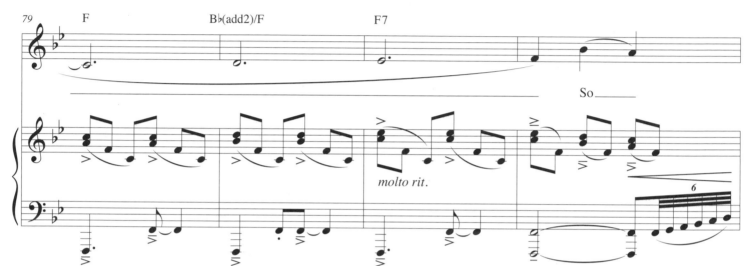

So_____

shine_____ on all the world_____

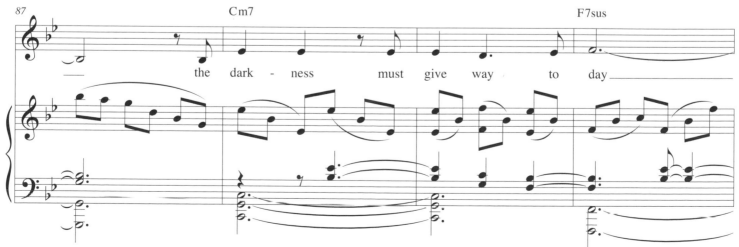

_____ the dark - ness must give way to day_____

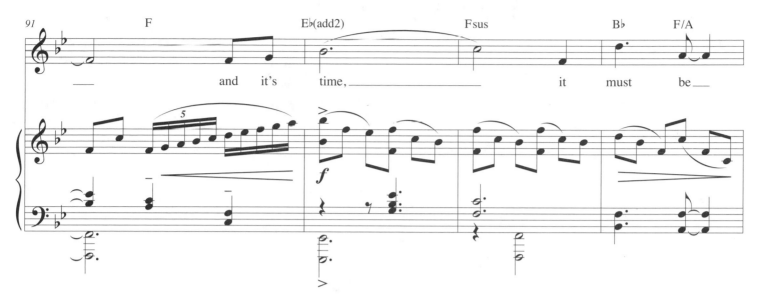

Poco ad lib.

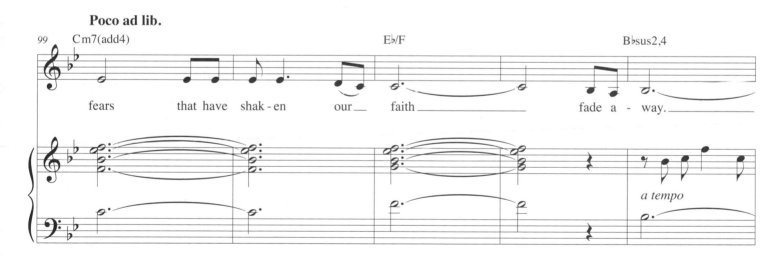

I STILL BELIEVE

Music and Lyrics by CHRISTOPHER SMITH
Arranged by Joseph Church

Moderately (♩ = 72)

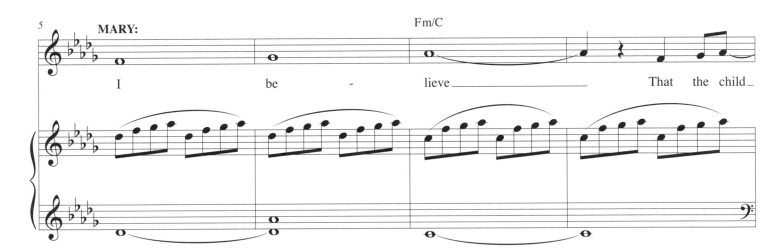

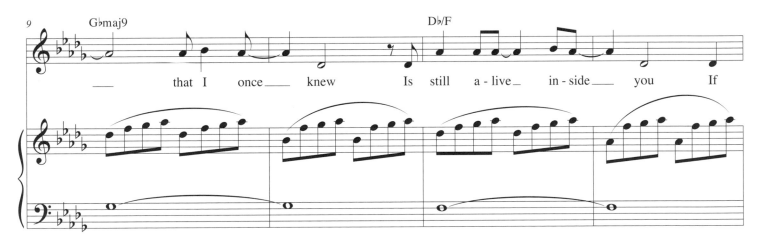

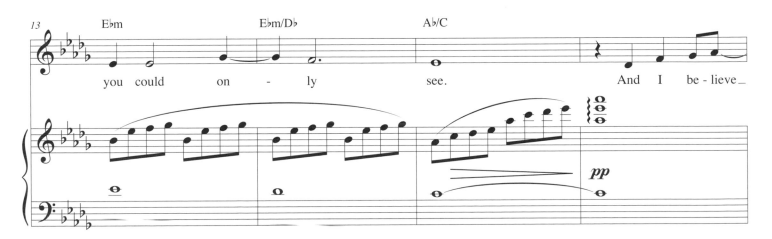

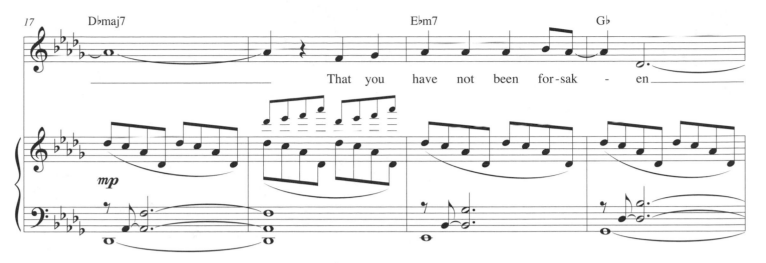

That you have not been for-sak - en

And this jour-ney you have tak - en Can some-how set

you free. For

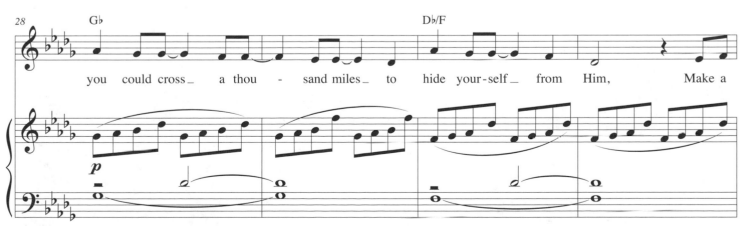

you could cross a thou - sand miles to hide your-self from Him, Make a

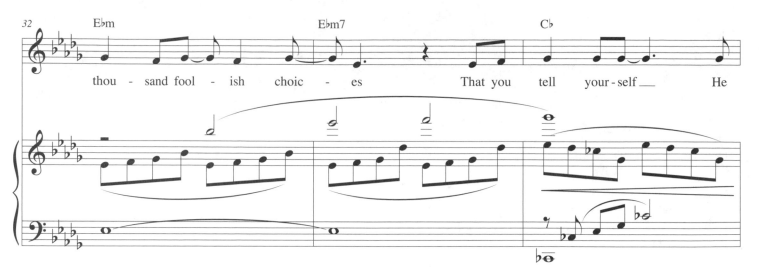

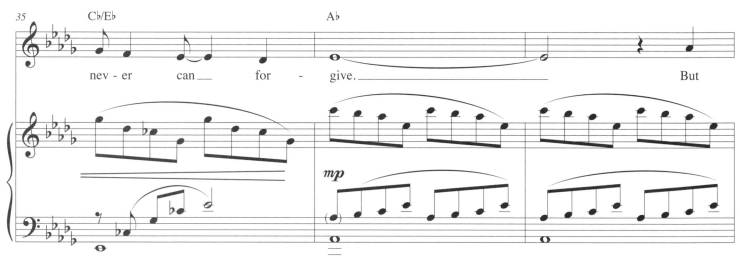

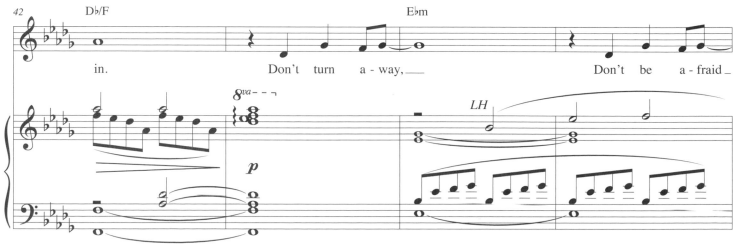

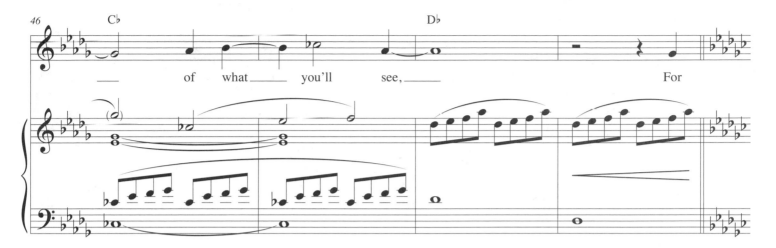

of what you'll see, For

all the things you once believed or thought you'd heard be -

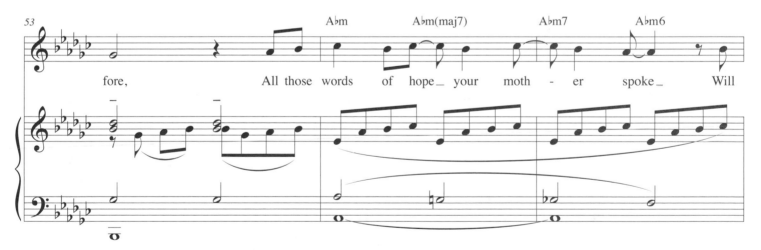

fore, All those words of hope your moth - er spoke Will

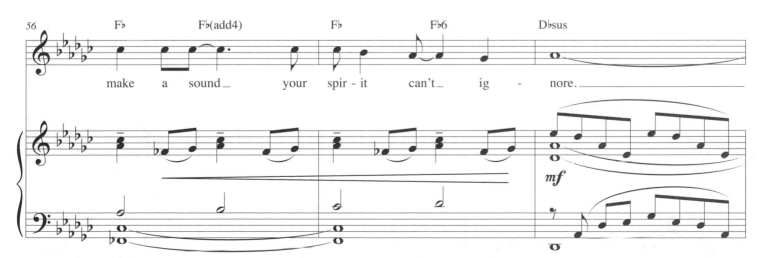

make a sound your spir - it can't ig - nore.

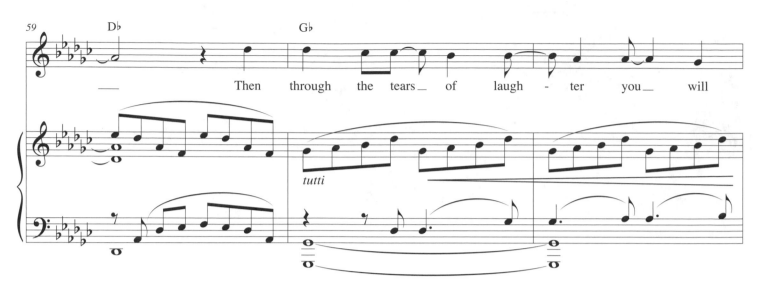

Then through the tears _ of laugh - ter you _ will

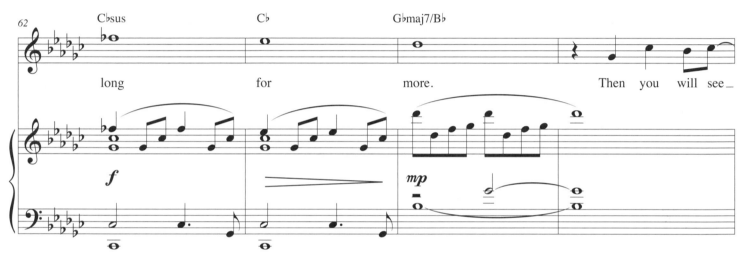

long for more. Then you will see _

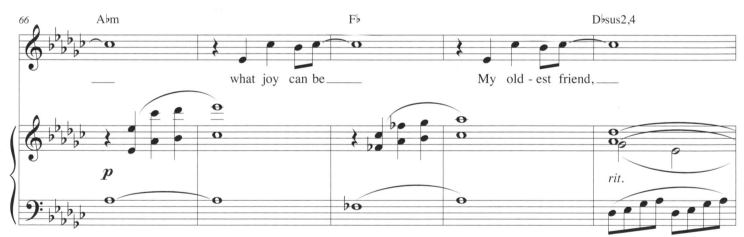

_ what joy can be _ My old - est friend, _

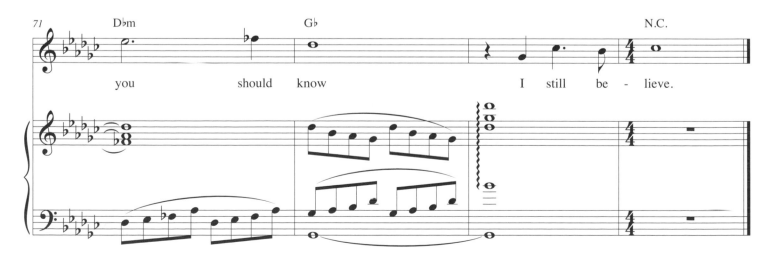

you should know I still be - lieve.

TESTIMONY

Music and Lyrics by CHRISTOPHER SMITH
Arranged by Joseph Church

mist on the bay____that is here and is gone____or as dreams fade a - way,____with the

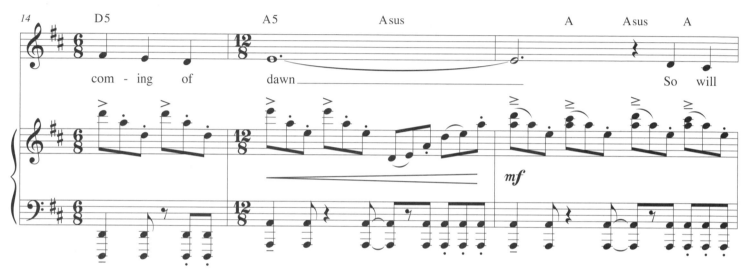

com - ing of dawn_____ So will

I. ____ I can

feel some - thing more_____ Stir-ring

deep in my soul A burn-ing for things I've ne-

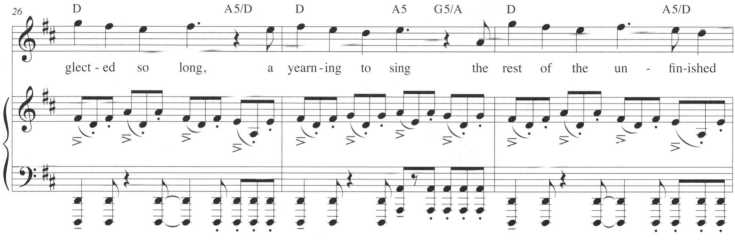

glect-ed so long, a yearn-ing to sing the rest of the un-fin-ished

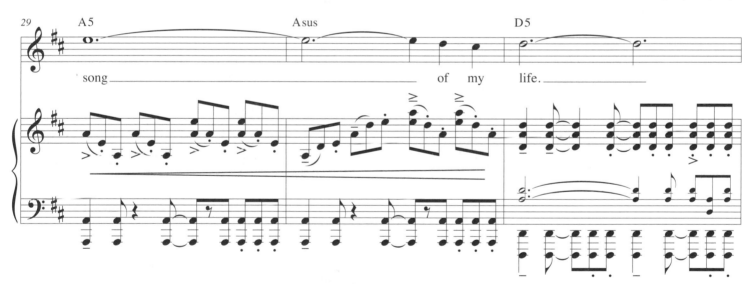

song of my life.

And the man that I was I cast up-on the fu-ry of the

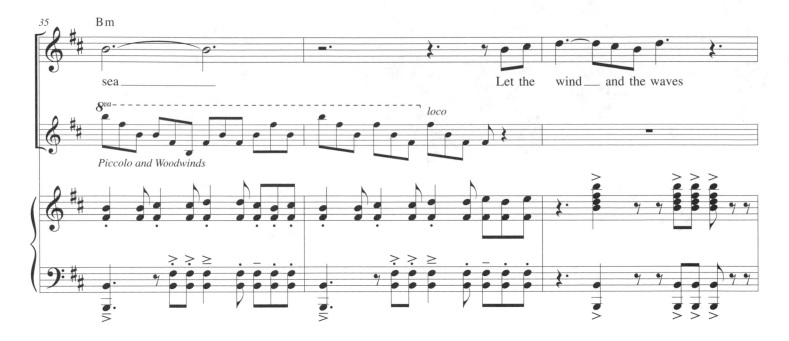

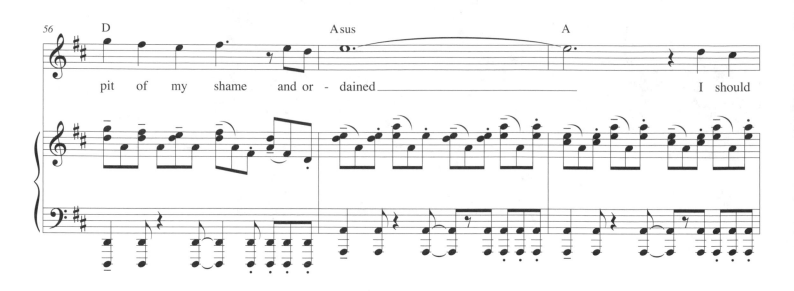

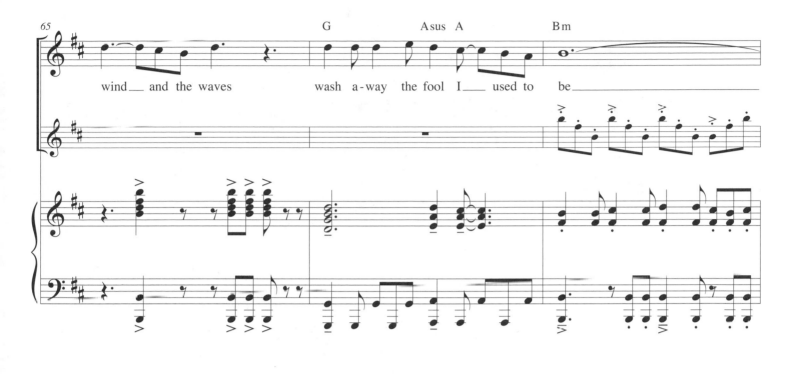

wind___ and the waves   wash a-way the fool I___ used to be___

_____ and I won't___ be a-shamed___ to stand and pro - claim I am

free _____ I am free _____

NOTHING THERE TO LOVE

Music and Lyrics by CHRISTOPHER SMITH
Arranged by Joseph Church
Additional arrangements by Dr. Joseph Ohrt

Tenderly (♩ = 72)

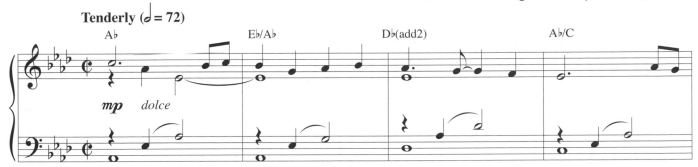

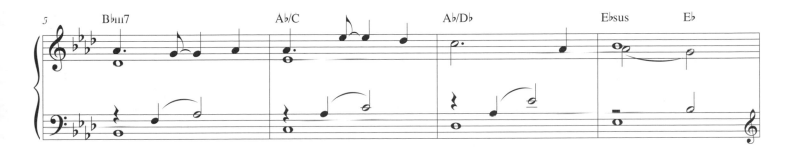

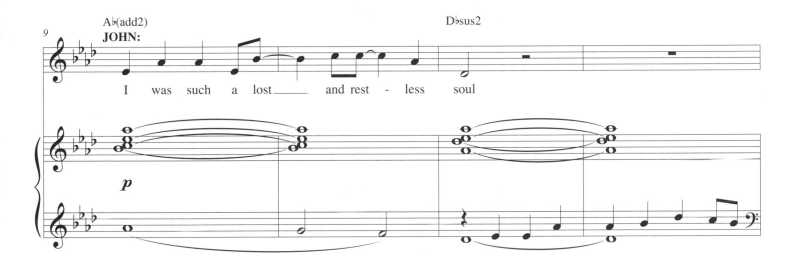

JOHN:
I was such a lost____ and rest - less soul

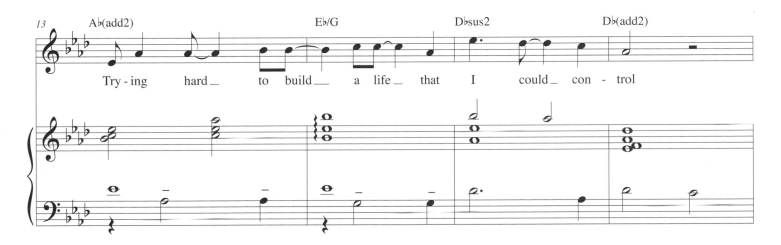

Try - ing hard____ to build____ a life____ that I could____ con - trol

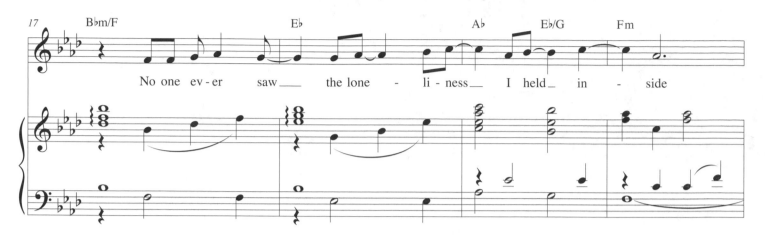

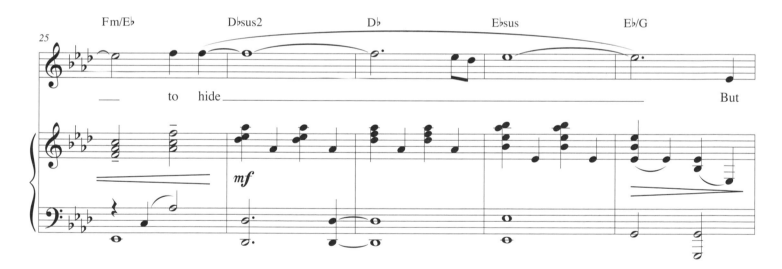

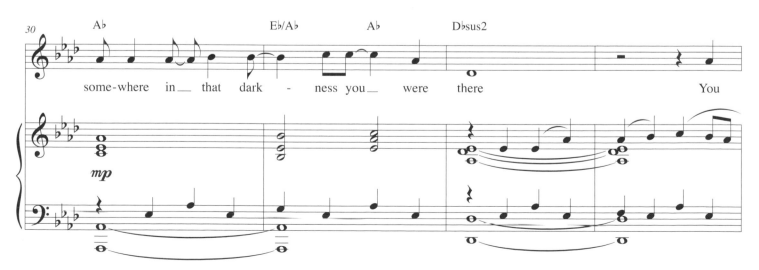

lis-tened to my mu - sic when the world did-n't care.

You're the on - ly one who saw be - yond the things I've done,

Who helped me see a vi - sion of the man I could

be - come

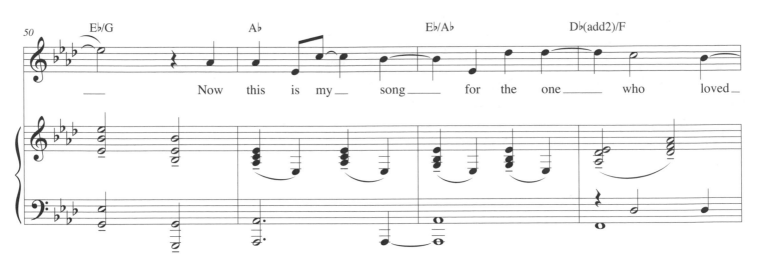

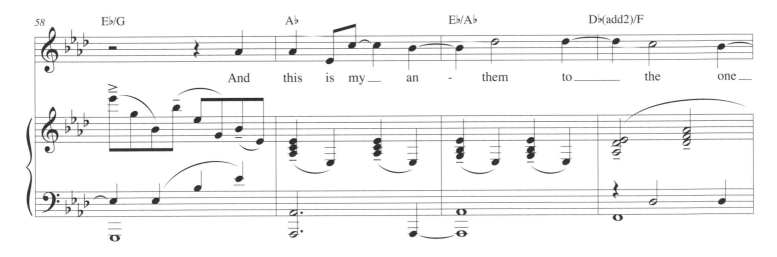

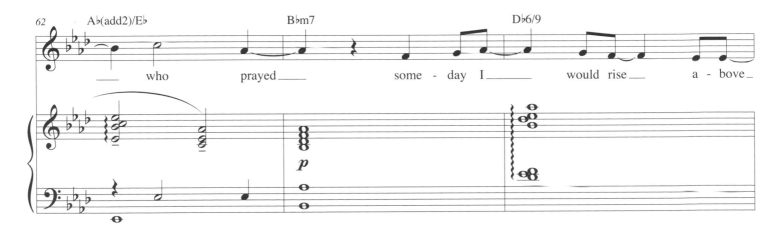

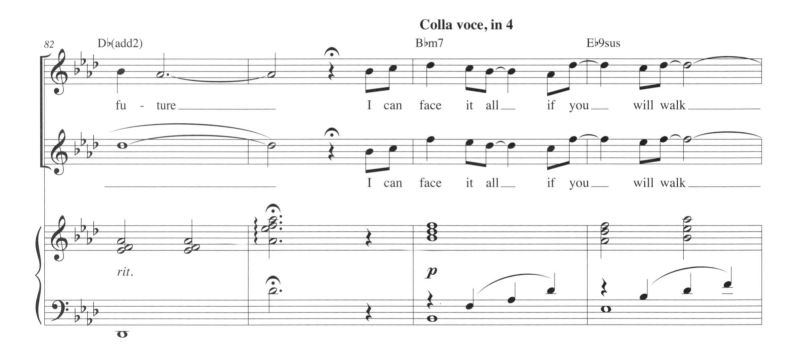

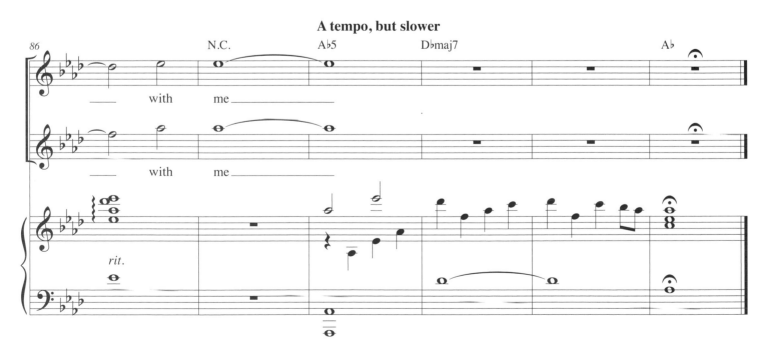

AMAZING GRACE

Music Traditional
Additional music by CHRISTOPHER SMITH
Lyrics by JOHN NEWTON
Arranged by Joseph Church
Additional arrangements by Karen Burgman

Simply and humbly, not too slow

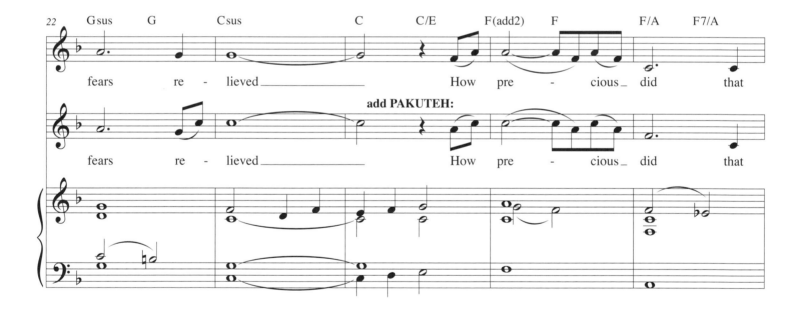

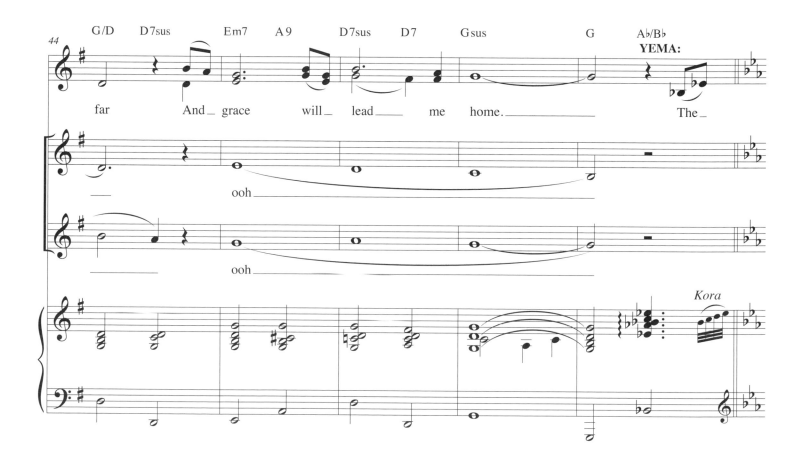

90

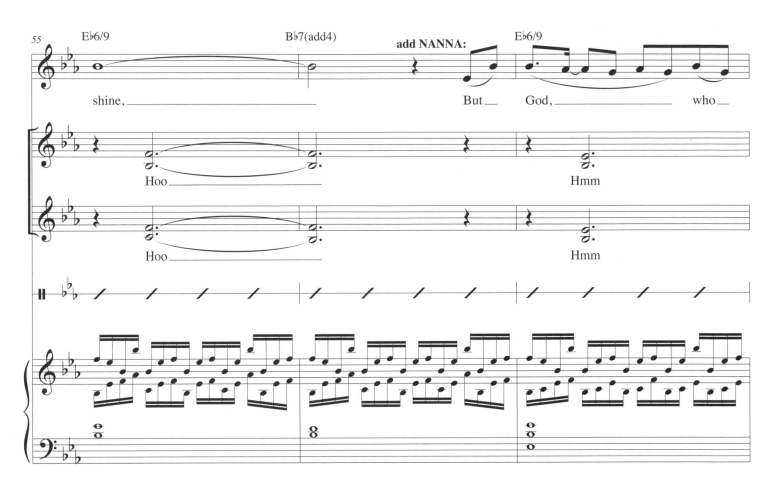

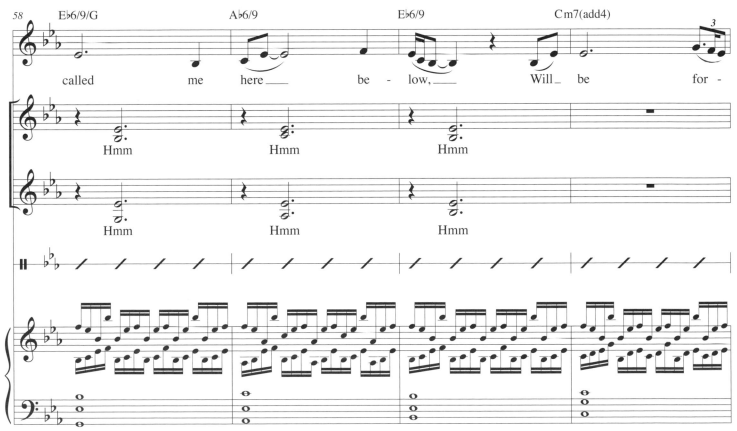

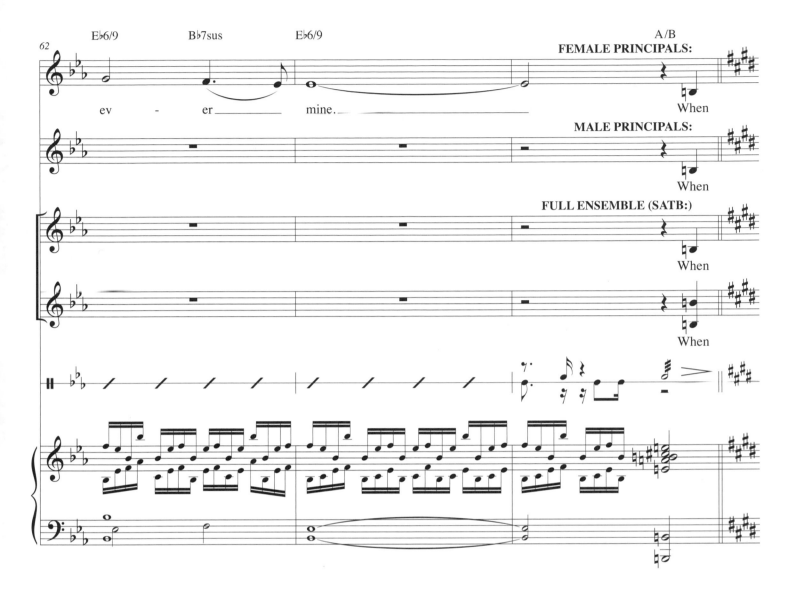

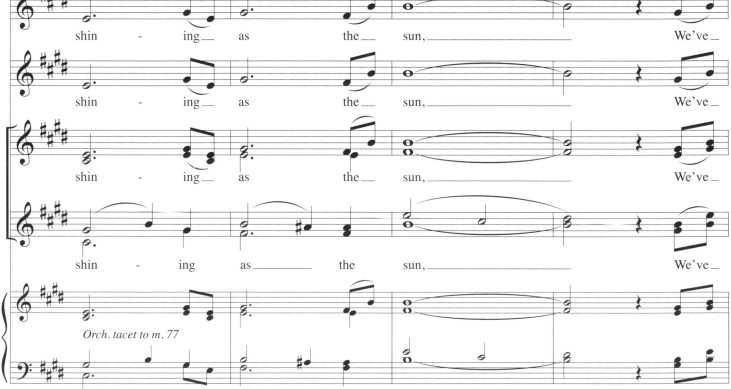

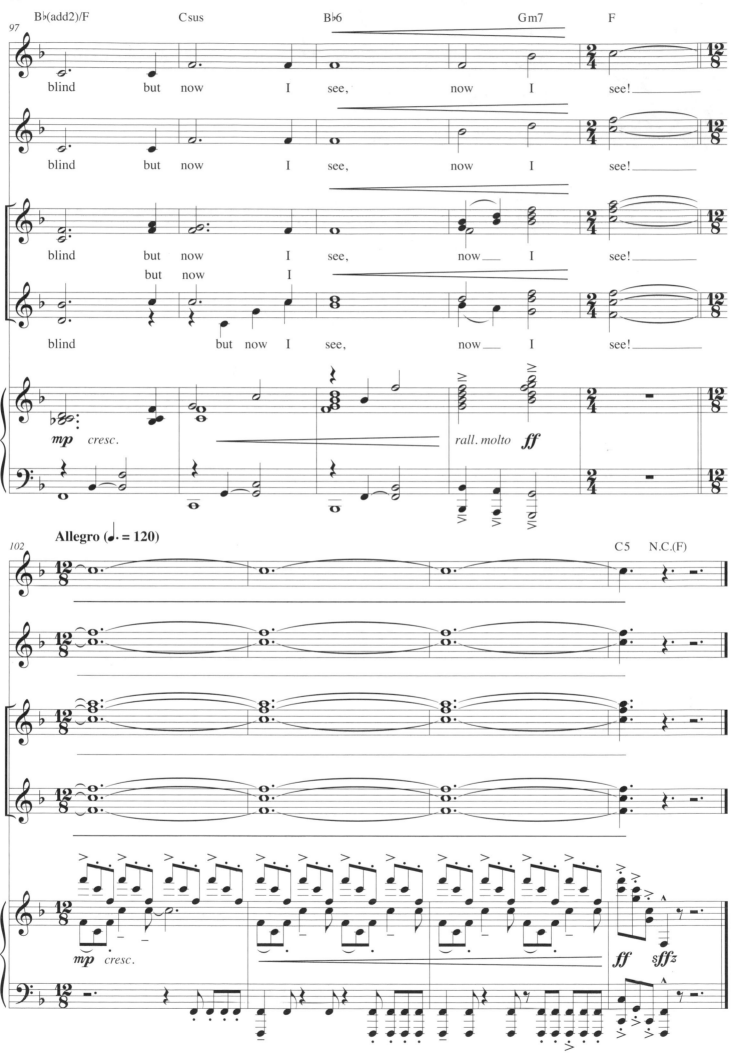